Don't Tax Me!

Don’t Tax Me!

An Introduction to Tax Strategies and Resolution

By

Carlos Ariel Then

For permissions, inquiries, or bulk purchases, please contact:
support@mrthen.biz
www.MrThen.biz

Published by Mr Then Consulting LLC
Providence, Rhode Island
Printed in the United States of America

Disclaimer

This book is for educational and informational purposes only. It is not intended as legal, tax, financial, or investment advice. While every effort has been made to ensure the accuracy of the content, the author and publisher make no guarantees or warranties, express or implied, and assume no responsibility for errors or omissions.

Tax laws change. Situations vary. Your cousin's refund story doesn't apply to you — go talk to a qualified tax professional for your specific needs. The strategies and perspectives shared in this book are based on the author's personal experience, research, and opinions developed over a decade in the industry. Translation: Don't try to sue me because you skipped the part where I said "consult a pro."

Table of Contents

Don’t Tax Me — Tax the Problem

Let’s cut the Bull Shit. (Excuse my French). Every year, millions of hardworking people hand over their cash to Uncle Sam like it’s some sacred ritual — blind, broke, and confused. Why? Because nobody taught them the tax game.

I always say, the more you know about how to play a game, the better you can play it, and the more likely you are to **win!**

The tax code wasn’t built to screw you — it was built to reward the people who *play it right*. But most folks are too distracted, too uninformed, or too afraid to even read it. Not you. Not anymore.

Don't Tax Me! It isn’t just another boring book about taxes. This is the wake-up call. The tax revolution. The unapologetic, straight-shooting blueprint you wish you had five years ago. I wrote this to empower entrepreneurs, hustlers, side gig champions, and everyday earners to stop being victims of "the system" and start using the system.

I’m not a CPA sitting in a glass tower. I’m in the trenches — fixing tax messes, building legacies, and showing people how to get out the financial matrix. If you’re tired of overpaying, under-planning, and always being one step behind — this book is your tool. Use it!

Fun Fact: We Didn’t Always Have an Income Tax

That's right. The United States didn’t even have a permanent income tax until 1913. Before that, we raised money through tariffs, property taxes, and whiskey taxes (yes, they taxed liquor — and folks *rioted*). The first income tax was introduced during the Civil War to fund the Union's war efforts, and it faded out. But when the **16th Amendment** passed in 1913, it gave Congress the power to tax individual incomes — and we've been paying ever since.

At first, it only hit the top 1% of earners. Today? You can barely breathe without the IRS wanting a piece. That's not a system — that's a trap. But like any trap, it only works if you don't see it.

Here's What They Don't Want You to Know:

- The tax code is over **75,000 pages** long — but only a small slice applies to you.
- Most of it? It's instructions and loopholes for businesses and investors.
- The wealthy don't "cheat" the system. They **understand it** better than you.

But now? So will you. If you're reading this, it means you're ready to *think differently*. You're done being a silent donor to the IRS. You're ready to start keeping more of your money, legally and strategically.
This isn't tax prep — this is *tax power*. Let's get to work.

The IRS Is Not Your Enemy

But It's Not Your Friend Either

Welcome to the Tax Game, Player 1

"If you don't understand how taxes work, you'll be working your whole life just to pay them." — Carlos Then

Let's Cut the CRAP...
Most people are scared of the IRS like it's some mafia boss hiding in their mailbox. And guess what? That's exactly how the system wants it. Keep you confused, intimidated, and complaint not by law, but by fear. Why do you think people came up with the phrase "Please don't tax me with your pricing"?
It's as if being "taxed" became 1:1 with being overcharged or being "burnt" on a deal.

Here's the truth:

- **Tax codes are written in favor of the informed.**
- **The wealthy aren't "cheating" — they're just using the rulebook better than you are.**
- **If you're overpaying in taxes, it's not because you're doing it wrong — it's because you're doing it blindly.**

A Quick History Lesson (Because Context is King)
Taxes weren't always this complicated. In fact, the **federal income tax** didn't even exist until **1913**, when the 16th Amendment was ratified. Before that? The US. funded itself mostly through **tariffs** and **excise taxes**. That's right — they were taxing booze and imports, not your paycheck.
But once they figured out, they could slice a piece off every dollar you earn, the government never looked back.
And to think, this country literally went to war at it's inception over taxes, but let's just forget about that... cause it's not important right?

- During **WWII**, the concept of "withholding" was introduced — aka the idea that the government should take your money **before you ever see it**.
- Now we've got over **70,000 pages** of tax code and most folks are still out here thinking H&R Block is the plug. (ha ha sorry I couldn't help myself)

The Game Is Rigged… Unless You Learn the Rules
You ever notice how the ultra-rich pay less in taxes than people working 9–5s? That's not a glitch — that's **design**.
W-2 income is the **most heavily taxed** form of income in the country.

Business income? Real estate income? Investment income? Those are taxed differently — and strategically.
The IRS doesn't reward hard work — it rewards **smart structuring**.

Here's what they never told you in school (because they were too busy teaching you the Pythagorean theorem):

Source of Income	**Tax Treatment**	**Who Wins?**
W-2 (Employee)	Taxed before you see it, few deductions	Government
1099 / Self-Employed	Taxed later, full deductions available	Hustlers who know the code
Business Owner	Control over expenses + tax strategy	Tax-advantaged boss moves
Investor / Real Estate	Depreciation + capital gains benefits	Wealthy + informed

Here's What This Book Will Do For You

If you're tired of:

- Working harder and keeping less
- Getting a refund and still feeling broke
- Living in fear of audits or penalties
- Never understanding how people *actually* pay little to no taxes…

Then welcome — you just unlocked the **cheat codes**.
This book is going to:

1. Teach you the rules they don't want you to learn
2. Break down taxes in plain English
3. Show you **how to structure your life like a business**
4. Walk you through deductions, credits, audits, resolutions, and more

No fluff. No legalese. Just power moves.

Real Talk Before We Dive In...

I'm not here to preach. I'm here to teach. This book won't make you a tax guru overnight, but it **will** make you dangerous — in a good way. You'll ask smarter questions. Make better money decisions. And most importantly, you'll never let a broken tax system break your pockets again.

So, buckle up.

Welcome to the side where we **play offense**, not just defense.

Let's make taxes make sense so you can save cents.

Understanding Your Tax Identity

Forget cats, trees, or your "aura" — this one's about your wallet.

“You can identify however you want — but the IRS only sees four types of people… and none of them care about your pronouns.” — Carlos Ariel Then

Identity Crisis? Not Here…
Look — these days people are identifying as everything from cats to celestial energy. And hey, if you want to meow at the moon or be a houseplant, that’s between you and your chakra.
But when it comes to taxes, the IRS couldn’t care less. There’s **no box for “tree” on your 1040.** There’s no deduction for emotional vibes. The system is **cold, calculated, and only cares about one thing: how your money flows.**

If you want to actually win this tax game, you need to stop identifying with **confusion**… and start identifying like a **strategist**.

This chapter is where we get real. No fluff. Just facts. You’re going to learn **how the IRS classifies you**, why it matters, and how to **shift your tax identity** to keep more of your hard-earned money.
Because whether you’re broke, ballin’, or building, there are only four **true tax identities**:

- W-2 Employee
- 1099 Contractor
- Sole Prop / LLC

- S-Corp / Partnership / Corporation

And those four doors lead to **four completely different tax worlds**.

Let's open each one…

The IRS Has You in a Box… Whether You Know It or Not

Imagine walking into a room with 4 doors. Each one leads to a different tax fate. The crazy part? Most people don't even know which door they walked through — but they **sure as hell** feel the consequences on April 15th.

Let's break down **the 4 main income identities**:

1. The W-2 Worker ***(AKA "The Employee")***

- **Form you get:** W-2
- **How you're taxed:** Automatically. Payroll taxes (Social Security + Medicare) and federal/state withheld *before* you get your money.
- **Write-offs allowed:** Basically none
- **Tax power:** Low
- **Who controls your money:** Uncle Sam does — first.

Translation: You're taxed like a robot. Work, get paid, get taxed, repeat. You can't write off the gas to work, your scrubs, or your laptop. The system is designed to keep you locked in the cycle.

2. The 1099 Hustler ***(AKA "Self-Employed / Contractor")***

- **Form you get:** 1099-NEC or 1099-K
- **How you're taxed:** No taxes withheld. You're in charge of paying quarterly or at year-end.
- **Write-offs allowed:** Tons — mileage, supplies, phone, internet, even part of your rent.

- **Tax power:** Moderate
- **Who controls your money:** You do. At first. But don't mess it up or the IRS comes knocking.

Pro tip: If you drive for Uber, do hair, run a side hustle, or freelance — this is you. But if you're not **tracking expenses**, you're losing big.

3. The LLC Owner *(AKA "You Took the First Boss Step")*

- **Form you get:** Could be 1099s, but the business gets its own identity (EIN).
- **How you're taxed:** Default is still **self-employment** unless you elect to be taxed as an S-Corp.
- **Write-offs allowed:** Same as 1099, but with more control and **legal protection.**
- **Tax power:** Strong
- **Who controls your money:** You — and you can pay yourself strategically.

Game changer: An LLC with *no tax election* is taxed the same as a sole prop but gives you legal benefits. Electing **S-Corp** status changes the tax game dramatically. That's a later chapter but just know: **LLC ≠ tax savings by default.**

4. The Business Entity *(No AKA just S-Corp / C-Corp / Partnership)*

- **Form you file:** 1120S (S-Corp), 1120 (C-Corp), or 1065 (Partnership)
- **How you're taxed:** Separately from your personal return — and you pay yourself via **W-2 or distributions**.
- **Write-offs allowed:** Maximum tax flexibility.
- **Tax power:** Boss level

- **Who controls your money:** You and your tax strategy.

Fun fact: An S-Corp can help you avoid **self-employment tax** on some of your income. That's 15.3% savings with the right setup. But don't try this alone — do it wrong and the IRS will spank you.
So... Which One Are You?

Here's a quick cheat sheet to find your identity:

If You...	You're Most Likely A...
Work full-time for a company	W-2 Employee
Do gigs, side hustles, freelance	1099 Contractor
Registered a business name	Sole Prop or LLC
Filed for an EIN + payroll setup	LLC or S-Corp
Split income with a partner	Partnership

Most people are stuck as W-2 employees, but **wishing** they had the tax breaks of a business owner. The only difference? **Knowledge and action.**

Identity = Opportunity (or Loss)

Every deduction, credit, loophole, and exemption is tied to how you're **categorized**.
If you're earning all your money through a W-2, you're playing the game in **hard mode**.
But the second you flip the script — even by starting a side hustle, freelancing, or forming an LLC — you unlock **massive tax strategy potential**.

Real Talk from Mr. Then

When I started doing taxes in college, I thought just filing fast and getting refunds was the flex. But over time I learned — the **real flex** is knowing how to structure your life, so your **income is efficient**, your **expenses are strategic**, and your **tax bill is tiny**.
So, before we dive deeper, you have to understand this:

- **How you earn determines how you're taxed**
- **How you're taxed determines how much you keep**
- **And how much you keep determines your wealth**

This is the foundation. Get it right, and everything else becomes easier.
Identity Check: Quick Tax Personality Quiz
You're one of these tax identities whether you like it or not. Let's figure it out before Uncle Sam does.
Pick the one that sounds most like you:

---

1. Your money comes in like this:
A. I get a paycheck every week or two with taxes already taken out.
B. I invoice people and get paid with no taxes withheld.
C. I have an LLC or side hustle that I treat like a real business.
D. I own a business, have payroll, or work with partners/shareholders.

---

2. When tax season comes, you:
A. Wait for your W-2 and pray for a refund.
B. Panic about your 1099 and how much you'll owe.
C. Deduct everything from your car to your couch.

D. Call your CPA and ask if the business qualifies for the QBI (Qualified Business Income) deduction.

---

3. You track expenses using:

A. My bank app when I remember.

B. My notes app... maybe.

C. QuickBooks or some spreadsheet I'm semi-proud of.

D. My bookkeeper does that. I just swipe my business card.

---

4. You feel taxes are:

A. Confusing. I just want to get it over with.

B. Unfair. Why am I punished for making money?

C. A game. And I'm learning how to win.

D. A tool. I use the system to my advantage.

Results:

Mostly A's – The Worker Bee (W-2 Employee)
You're on payroll. Taxes get snatched before you even see them. You *might* get a refund if the math favors you. Deductions? Minimal. Power? Low. But don't worry — we'll show you how to level up.

Mostly B's – The Hustler (1099 Independent Contractor)
You eat what you kill. You've got freedom, but also the IRS breathing down your neck. You need strategy, structure, and receipts. This book is about to be your new best friend.

Mostly C's – The Emerging Boss (LLC or Sole Prop)
You've started thinking like a business. Maybe you're

claiming your mileage, maybe you're writing off your Wi-Fi. Either way, you're halfway in. We're about to take you all the way.

Mostly D's – The Tax Savage (S-Corp or Partnership Owner)

You've got entities, payroll, maybe even a SEP IRA. You're in the tax matrix and moving like a boss. But there's still more juice to squeeze — and we're about to press it.

Now that you know who you are, let's get into what you can actually **do** about it.

Ready for some straight-up tax game?

Let's dive into Chapter 3 — *The Tax System Is Not Your Friend (But You Can Still Beat It)*

The Tax System Isn't made for you

But that doesn't mean you can't win, You can still beat them.

You see, the problem is... they're playing chess. You've been playing Uno.

"Don't bring a knife to a tax fight. Bring receipts and strategy." — Carlos Then

Let's Talk Facts, Not Feelings

The IRS doesn't care about your struggle. It doesn't care if your rent went up, your paycheck stayed the same, or that you overpaid for TurboTax and still ended up confused.

All it cares about is numbers. Inputs. Outputs. Line 1 through Line 37.

And guess what? **You've probably been overpaying your whole adult life.**

Why? Because the tax system is designed that way — **to favor structure, not labor.**

If you just "go with the flow," that flow leads to a smaller refund, a bigger bill, and no generational wealth.

So let me break this down for you the way your teachers never did.

How the IRS Really Works (The Oversimplified Truth)

Here's how the system is structured:

1. **You earn income**
2. **You report it** on a tax return (Form 1040)
3. The government checks if you qualify for any:
    - Deductions (reduces taxable income)
    - Credits (reduces tax owed)

    - Exemptions (not as common post-2018)
4. Then it calculates your tax **based on what's left**
5. If you paid in more than you owe? **Refund.**
   Paid in less? **You Owe**.

Simple right? Not really.

Because what most people miss is **where your money is coming from, and what that means for taxes.** We hit on it last chapter. But now we're going to go deeper.

Income Is Not Just Income (It's How It's Labeled)

You could earn $50,000 as a W-2 employee or $50,000 through your LLC and owe two totally different amounts in taxes.

Let's visualize it:

Income Type	Tax Impact
W-2	Full payroll tax + income tax. No write-offs.
1099/Sole Prop	Self-employment tax + income tax, **but full deductions** available.
S-Corp	Wages taxed like W-2, but profits (distributions) often escape self-employment tax.
Real Estate Rental	Can show a "loss" on paper thanks to depreciation, even while making money.
Investments	Long-term capital gains taxed lower than your job. Some even **tax-free**.

The government doesn't punish income.

It punishes **how your income is structured.**

Here's Why Most People Overpay

- They rely on a refund as a savings account
- They don't understand the **difference between tax prep and tax planning**
- They don't track expenses all year
- They're afraid of the IRS — so they stay passive

Let me be clear:
A refund is not a bonus. It's a loan, It's your own money, coming back without interest, and sometimes you don't even get all of it back.
Real Strategy: Income Shifting
This is where bosses win.
Instead of earning all your money through one source, you **split** it across different buckets — wages, business income, investments, rental income, etc.
It's what rich people do. And they don't wait until March to plan. They start in January.
They:

- Set up LLCs
- Elect S-Corp status
- Contribute to retirement accounts
- Track business mileage
- Lease vehicles strategically
- Invest in real estate for write-offs
- Use family and kids in the business legally

This isn't rocket science. It's **tax code** — and it's written for those who learn it.
Real Talk with Mr. Then
When I started doing taxes in college, I was just chasing refunds. I thought the bigger the number on the screen, the better I did. But once I got into the game for real — I realized the **goal isn't the refund**. The goal is to pay the **least amount legally** and build long-term wealth.
Most of my clients don't have tax problems — they have identity problems. They're moving like workers, not wealth builders.
Coming Up in Chapter 4…
"The Holy Trinity of Deductions" — Home, Vehicle, and Meals. Learn them. Leverage them. Live by them.
You're about to unlock the most slept-on section of the tax code — the part that makes *you* the boss.

That ends now. But before that, let me show you how two people can earn the same amount and pay different amounts.

Tax Bill Breakdown: Same Income, Different Outcome (2025 Numbers)

Let's compare two people who both make **$60,000**, but one is a **W-2 employee**, and the other is a **1099/LLC hustler** who knows the game.

	W-2 Worker	**1099/LLC Hustler**
Gross Income	$60,000	$60,000
Standard Deduction	-$15,000 (Single, 2025)	-$15,000
Taxable Income	$45,000	$45,000
Federal Income Tax	~$5,100	~$5,100
Payroll / SE Tax	~$4,590 withheld	~$9,180 (15.3% SE tax)
Business Deductions	None	$18,000 in real write-offs
Revised Taxable Income	$45,000	$27,000
Adjusted Total Tax	~$9,690	~$6,100
Net Tax Savings	$0	**~$3,590 in savings**

Let's Break It Down:

- **The W-2 Worker** has **no control** over taxes — everything's withheld before they even touch their money.
- **The 1099 Hustler** takes control. They deduct:
    - Mileage
    - Cell phone
    - Home office
    - Laptop & gear
    - Meals
    - Insurance

All **legal. All IRS-approved. All money-saving.**

Wake-Up Call:
"The system is designed to reward structure, not hustle. Unless you structure your hustle."
This is how rich people pay less on **$600,000** than most W-2 earners do on **$60,000**. The game isn't rigged — you just weren't given the rule-book. Until now.

Coming Up: Chapter 4 — The Holy Trinity of Deductions But first let's take a look at the most common deductions.
Get ready to unlock IRS-proof write-offs that change the game:
Home. Vehicle. Meals. These three alone can legally erase thousands from your tax bill. Let's go!

Top 10 Tax-Deductible Expenses

If you spend it for the biz, document it, and make it make sense — you can likely write it off.

---

1. **Mileage & Vehicle Expenses**

- Track your **business miles** (keep a log or use an app like MileIQ or Everlance)
- OR deduct actual expenses like gas, maintenance, insurance, and car loan interest (business-use %)

Mr. Then Tip: Don't try to deduct a brand-new Benz at 100% if you only DoorDash on weekends. Be real.

---

2. **Home Office**

- A dedicated workspace = major tax savings
- Use **simplified method** ($5/sq ft up to 300 sq ft) or actual expenses (rent, utilities, internet, insurance, etc.)

Bonus Tip: Painting your office = **100% deductible direct expense**

---

3. **Cell Phone & Internet**

- If you use your phone or Wi-Fi for business (which you do), write off the **business-use %**

75% of your $100/month phone bill = $75 x 12 = $900 deduction

Just don't say TikTok is "client research" if you're just scrolling memes.

---

4. **Meals (50% Deductible)**

- Business meals while traveling, meeting clients, or doing biz-related work
- Must be **documented** with who, what, when, and why

Lunch with your business partner = Good to Go!
Pizza with your ex = No Go! (unless they're your CFO)

---

5. **Marketing & Advertising**

- Business cards, Instagram ads, branded hoodies, flyers, promo giveaways, website, etc.

Real Game: That Canva Pro subscription? Yep. Write it off.

---

6. **Supplies & Equipment**

- Pens, planners, chargers, ring lights, tools, camera gear, printers — if you use it for business, it's deductible.

□ Bought a printer? Deduct it. Depreciate it? Maybe. We'll cover that in Chapter 6.

---

7. **Education & Training**

- Courses, workshops, books (like this one), coaching — if it **improves your business skills**, it's deductible.

TurboTax Academy? Yes.
"How to Be a Sugar Baby 101"? Sorry, no.

---

8. **Insurance**

- Business insurance, liability coverage, E&O insurance
- **Self-employed health insurance** premiums (if not through a marketplace)

Protection is power — and yes, the IRS supports it.

---

9. **Travel**

- Flights, hotels, Airbnbs, Ubers, tolls — if it's business-related, it's likely deductible.

Just make sure you're not calling that "Vegas with the bros" a "team-building retreat" unless they're truly on payroll.

---

10. **Professional Services**

- Tax prep, bookkeeping, legal help, business consulting

Paid someone to help you file taxes? Boom. Write it off.

Paid your cousin with Zelle and no receipt? Nope. That's just love.

Bonus Mr. Then Advice:
"If you can prove it, track it, and justify it — you can probably deduct it."
Pair this cheat sheet with:

- A receipts folder (digital or physical)
- Monthly bookkeeping check-ins
- A real tax pro who knows how to play offense

The Holy Trinity of Deductions

Home. Vehicle. Meals.

The three write-offs that Uncle Sam secretly *expects* you to miss.

"They say don't mix business with pleasure — but if you do it right, you can at least deduct part of the pleasure." — Carlos Then

---

Intro: Stop Paying for Stuff Twice

You ever sit down to do your taxes and think, "Where the f*ck did all my money go?"

Answer:

- Some went to Starbucks
- Some went to DoorDash
- Some went to bills
- And most of it went to the government

But here's what I'm about to teach you:

If you're using your **home, vehicle, or eating out** for business — the tax code gives you permission to **claim part of that life back.**

You just have to know **how to track it, write it off, and back it up**.

---

1. The Home Office Deduction

Who qualifies:

- You're self-employed, 1099, or have a business (LLC, etc.)
- You use part of your home **exclusively and regularly** for business
- Not applicable to regular W-2 workers (sorry, teachers)

How it works:

You've got two options:

A. Simplified Method

- $5 per square foot
- Max 300 sq ft = **$1,500 deduction**

B. Actual Expenses Method

You calculate the % of your home used for business

Example:

- 120 sq ft / 2,000 sq ft = 6%
- You can write off 6% of:
  - Rent or mortgage interest
  - Utilities
  - Insurance
  - Repairs
  - Property taxes

Mr. Then Pro Tip:

Painted your office? Bought a desk or chair? That's a **direct expense** — not prorated. Write that off at **100%**.

---

2. Vehicle Expenses

Who qualifies:

If you **drive for business**, whether you're DoorDashing, real estating, mobile notary-ing, or just driving to meet a client — you can deduct mileage or actual expenses.

Two methods (pick one — not both):

A. Standard Mileage Rate

- 2025: Let's say 67 cents/mile
- Drive 5,000 business miles → 5,000 x $0.67 = **$3,350 deduction**
  (Must have a mileage log or app)

B. Actual Expenses

- Gas, oil, tires, insurance, registration, maintenance, car washes, lease payments, car loan interest, depreciation
- Multiply **total expenses** by your **business-use %** (based on mileage)

Mr. Then Pro Tip:
If you buy a car **over 6,000 lbs**, you may qualify for **bonus depreciation or Section 179** — aka write off a **huge chunk** in year one.

---

3. Meals
Who qualifies:
If you're eating while traveling for business, meeting clients, or handling business-related activities — you can likely write off 50% of the meal.
Rules:

- **50% deductible** (unless IRS changes it — used to be 100% during COVID)
- Must be business-related
- Keep receipts and **write on the back who it was with and why**

Examples:

- Lunch with a client = **Good to go!**
- Dinner after a full day at a conference = **Good to go!**
- Taco Bell while binge-watching Netflix = **No go!** (unless Netflix is your content research)

Mr. Then Pro Tip:
Create a habit: **Snap a pic of every receipt and email it to yourself** with a subject line like: "MEAL – John – Business planning – $32"

Why These 3 Matter So Much
Because most of y'all are already:

- Living in your house
- Driving your car
- Eating food

But only the tax-savvy are **getting reimbursed by the government** for doing it in connection with their hustle.

This chapter alone could save you **$5,000 – $15,000** a year if you apply it right.

Real Talk Wrap-Up:
"You already spend the money. Now learn how to get some of it back."
The IRS is counting on you to forget receipts, guess mileage, and skip the details. But now you know better. Track it. Deduct it. And when in doubt — consult a pro (a real one, not your cousin who filed on his phone in a barbershop).

Deduction Tracking Checklist

Track It. Prove It. Deduct It.

"If you can't prove it, you can't deduct it. Keep your receipts like you keep your money — tight." — Carlos Then

---

DAILY / WEEKLY DEDUCTIONS TO TRACK:

Expense Type	Track This Info	Receipt Needed?
Meals	Who, What, Where, Why (write on the receipt)	YES
Gas / Mileage	Date, Miles, Business Purpose	YES (Log or App)
Parking / Tolls	Date, Location, Event/Meeting Name	YES
Online Ads	Platform, Purpose (Facebook, Google, etc.)	YES
Business Supplies	Item Name, Purpose, Date of Use	YES
Tips / Gratuity	Only if business-related meals/travel	YES (on receipt)

MONTHLY EXPENSES TO TRACK:

Expense Type	Track This Info	Receipt Needed?
Home Office	Square footage used, full home sq. ft.	YES (for expenses)
Rent / Mortgage Interest	Monthly amount, percentage used for business	YES (Statement)
Utilities	Electric, Water, Internet – monthly amount	YES
Cell Phone Bill	% used for business, plan details	YES
Software/Apps	Name, Cost, Purpose (Canva, QuickBooks, etc.)	YES
Subscriptions	Biz-related only (Mailchimp, Zoom, CRMs)	YES
Insurance	Business or health insurance premiums	YES

VEHICLE EXPENSES (If Using Actual Expense Method):

Expense Type	Track This Info	Receipt Needed?
Gas	Date, Gallons, Station	YES

Expense Type	Track This Info	Receipt Needed?
Oil Changes	Date, Shop, Cost	YES
Car Insurance	Annual Premium, Coverage Dates	YES
Repairs / Tires	Type of repair, Date, Business use %	YES
Loan Interest	Lender, Year-End Statement	YES
Depreciation	Car value, Purchase date, Biz use %	YES (Bill of sale/title)

ANNUAL EXPENSES TO TRACK:

Expense Type	Track This Info	Receipt Needed?
Tax Prep	Who filed for you, Cost	YES
Legal or Consulting Fees	Names, Services Provided	YES
Courses / Education	Course name, Provider, Business Purpose	YES
Marketing Materials	Printing, Design, Website Updates	YES
Gifts (under $25)	Client Name, Occasion	YES
Professional Licenses	Renewal Fees, Dates	YES

Mr. Then's Real Talk Reminders:

Use an app like **QuickBooks, Wave, or Notion** to organize this

Snap pics of receipts ASAP — email them to yourself w/ subject line: *"Biz Expense – [category] – [date]"*

Keep **digital + backup folder** (Google Drive or physical file)

Don't guess. **If it's blurry, don't deduct it.**

Pro Move: Add this list to your **monthly calendar** or accountability routine. Deduction tracking isn't once a year — it's all year.

Business or Hobby? The IRS Smell Test

*If it looks like a hobby, smells like a hobby… they're not letting you deduct sh*t.*

"The IRS doesn't care what you call it — they care how you run it." — Carlos Then

---

Let's Get Something Straight:
Not everything that makes money is a business.
And not everything that loses money is a hobby.
But when the IRS comes knocking? You better know **which one you're running.**
So many people try to write off:

- That "side hustle" they haven't promoted in 9 months
- That one t-shirt sale they made on Shopify
- Or the podcast they recorded in their cousin's basement — once

And then they wonder why they get flagged for an audit.

IRS Rule 1: You Can't Deduct Losses From a Hobby
You can make money from a hobby — cool. But **you can't claim losses or deductions** the same way you can from a business. The IRS calls this the **"Hobby Loss Rule"** and they're not playing with it.
Translation: If you're not treating your hustle like a real business, the IRS won't either.

What Makes It a Real Business? Here's the IRS Smell Test

There are **9 factors** the IRS uses to decide if you're running a legit business or just vibing with your Venmo account.

The IRS "Smell Test" – Do You:

1. **Run it in a businesslike manner?**
   Separate bank account? Recordkeeping? Receipts?
2. **Have expertise or seek advisors?**
   You study your industry or get help (books, coaching, etc.)
3. **Put in time and effort to make it profitable?**
   You're actually trying to grow it — not just "dabbling."
4. **Depend on the income for survival?**
   It's more than a hobby — you need/want it to produce.
5. **Have a history of making a profit?**
   Even a little. Doesn't need to be much — just needs to be **intentional**.
6. **Have occasional profits?**
   You've shown some wins — even if it's inconsistent.
7. **Expect asset appreciation?**
   You're building something with value (brand, content, inventory, etc.)
8. **Change methods to improve profitability?**
   You adapt, tweak, invest, or upgrade.
9. **Act like other successful businesses in your field?**
   You're doing what real pros do — not winging it.

The 3-Year Rule (That Most People Screw Up)
If you don't show **a profit in at least 3 out of 5 years**, the IRS *might* label your biz as a hobby.

Now listen — this rule isn't automatic. You can still defend your business, but you better have your ducks in a row:

- Contracts
- Invoices
- Proof of effort
- Marketing strategies
- Equipment & investments

If it looks like you're just trying to write off vacations and your laptop… they'll shut it down **fast.**

Real Examples: Business vs. Hobby

Scenario	Hobby or Business?	Why
Selling T-shirts online once in a while	Hobby	No consistent effort, no biz setup
Driving Uber part-time and tracking mileage	Business	1099, profit motive, records
Buying a camera and saying you're a "content creator" but only posting selfies	Hobby	No biz model, no income, no plan
Creating a planner brand, marketing on IG, reinvesting profits	Business	Intent, promotion, structure

---

Mr. Then Real Talk:
"If you want IRS respect, you got to move like a boss — even when your biz is still small."
I've seen people **scared to call their business a business** until it makes big money. That's backward

thinking.
You **start with structure**, then the money catches up.

Boss Moves Checklist — Make Sure Your Business:
Has a business bank account
Has an EIN (Employer Identification Number)
Tracks income & expenses
Files taxes yearly (even at a loss!)
Has a simple website or IG page
Has a plan — even a basic one
Isn't just "vibes and invoices"

Bottom Line:
Don't play audit roulette.
If you want tax benefits, move like a business. If it's just for fun — cool. Just don't try to write it off.

Write It Off or Wipe It Out

What you can legally deduct — and what'll get you cooked. (As the kids say nowadays)

"You don't get to just write off your lifestyle. You write off what's ordinary, necessary, and documented."

Welcome to the Deduction Deep Dive
Everybody loves saying, "I'm writing that off," but 90% of people couldn't tell you what that actually means. Spoiler alert: the IRS has receipts, systems, and red flags in place to catch the sloppy ones.
In this chapter, I'm going to give you the real rules, the gray areas, and the strategies to write off like a boss — not a clown.

What Does "Write-Off" Really Mean?
When you deduct something from your taxes, you're reducing your **taxable income** — not your actual taxes dollar for dollar.
Here's the play:

- You earn $80,000
- You have $20,000 in qualified business deductions
- You're only taxed on $60,000

The **lower your taxable income**, the less you owe in taxes. That's how wealthy people keep more of what they make. Not by hiding income — but by strategically writing off expenses the right way.

The IRS Standard: "Ordinary and Necessary"
If you take nothing else from this chapter, remember these two words.

Ordinary: Common in your type of business
Necessary: Helpful and appropriate for your business
This definition is flexible depending on your industry. What's ordinary for a fitness coach might not fly for a notary. You've got to be able to connect the dots — and back it up.

Common Deductions You Should Know

Here's a breakdown of what most self-employed people can legally deduct — assuming they're keeping proper records and using it for business.

1. Advertising and Marketing

Websites, flyers, Instagram ads, business cards, branding materials

2. Vehicle Expenses

Mileage OR actual expenses (gas, insurance, repairs, depreciation). Must be tracked carefully.

3. Business Meals

50% deductible if directly related to business. Keep details of who you met with and why.

4. Home Office

Deduct a portion of rent, mortgage interest, utilities, internet if used exclusively for business.

5. Cell Phone and Internet

Business-use portion. Don't try to write off your entire bill unless it's 100% business.

6. Office Supplies and Equipment

Printers, paper, monitors, ring lights, planners, pens, software

7. Professional Services

Legal, accounting, tax prep, business consulting

8. Business Travel

Flights, hotels, car rentals, meals while traveling for work. Must have a business reason.

9. Insurance

Business insurance, health insurance if self-employed

10. Continuing Education
Books, courses, certifications that improve your current business or trade

---

Deductions That Get You Flagged (or Denied)
Some things people *think* they can write off, but often cross the line.

Clothing
Unless it's a uniform or has branding that can't be worn casually, it's not deductible.

Personal travel disguised as business
If you "attended a webinar" while on a cruise, but didn't have a legit business agenda, that's a no.

Family dinners
Meals with your kids don't count as team meetings. Stop playing.

Your whole rent or mortgage
You can't deduct your full rent just because you answer emails from your couch.

Documentation Is Non-Negotiable
The IRS doesn't need a reason to question your deductions. All it takes is one audit. If you can't prove it, they can deny it — and hit you with penalties.
You need:

- Receipts (paper or digital)
- Date, amount, business purpose
- Mileage logs or app tracking
- Invoices or proof of income to match the expense
- Clear separation between personal and business spending

When to Use Depreciation
Some things (like vehicles, computers, furniture, cameras) can't be deducted all at once — especially if they cost more than a few thousand dollars.

This is where depreciation comes in. It spreads the deduction over several years.
Or, if the situation fits, you might use **Section 179** or **bonus depreciation** to deduct more in year one.
Talk to your tax pro. This is one of the most powerful tools when done right — and one of the most dangerous when done wrong.

Pro Tip: Don't Get Greedy, Get Smart
Writing off every dollar of your lifestyle isn't strategy — it's a setup. Focus on writing off what you can defend, not what you think you can get away with.
The people who get burned in audits aren't the ones who deducted real business meals or their Canva subscription. It's the ones who wrote off Cancun as a "branding retreat" and can't prove anything.

Closing Words
Writing it off is a privilege that comes with structure and discipline. The better your system, the more you'll legally keep.
If you're not tracking, you're losing.
If you're not planning, you're paying.
And if you're not writing off smart, you're wiping out your own profits.
Write-Off Tracker Template
Track It. Prove It. Deduct It.
Keep your money by keeping your records.

INSTRUCTIONS:
Use this table weekly or monthly. For digital users, use a spreadsheet with the same headings. For paper users — print a similar page or recreate it in your planner.
The IRS doesn't care how you track it, just that you do.

Date	Vendor / Store / Platform	Item or Service Purchased	Amount	Business Purpose / Notes	Category (Meals, Mileage, Office, etc.)	Receipt Saved? (Y/N)

Suggested Categories:

- **Marketing & Ads**
- **Meals & Entertainment**
- **Office Supplies**
- **Home Office**
- **Vehicle / Mileage**
- **Professional Services**
- **Software & Subscriptions**
- **Travel**
- **Education / Courses**
- **Utilities & Internet**

Monthly Summary Section:

- **Total Deductions This Month: $____________**
- **Receipts Missing: ______________**
- **Follow-Ups / Clarifications Needed: ______________**

Mr. Then's Tips for Using This Like a Pro:

- Save digital receipts in a dedicated folder labeled by **month + category**

- Snap a photo of every paper receipt as soon as possible and email it to yourself
- Use simple subject lines like: "Receipt – Canva Pro – Jan 3 – Marketing"
- Review this log at the **end of each month** and tally totals per category
- Use it during tax season to make your filing easy — or hand it to your tax pro

Smart Structuring

Start where you are — but structure like you've already made it.

"It's not about how big your business is — it's about how seriously you treat it."

The Problem With 'I Just Started'
Too many people wait until they're "making real money" to structure their business. That's backwards. You don't wait for the money to come — you build the system that **brings in and protects** the money before it lands.
No matter what stage you're in — just getting started or scaling up — you need to structure correctly from the start.
Let's break it down.

Step 1: What Counts as a Business?
According to the IRS, if you're engaged in an activity with the **intention of making a profit**, it can be a business.
You don't need to:

- Have an LLC (yet)
- Make six figures
- Be full-time

You *do* need to:

- Track income and expenses
- Have a plan to grow
- Treat it like it matters

If you made a single dollar offering a service, selling something, or freelancing — congratulations, you're a business. Now act like one.

Step 2: Start-Up Costs — What You Can Deduct

The IRS allows you to deduct up to **$5,000** of business **start-up costs** and $5,000 in **organizational costs** in your first year of business.

What's included:

- Branding, logos, and design
- Website setup
- Equipment and tools
- Legal and tax consultations
- Marketing and research
- Initial supplies
- Software and subscriptions

If your start-up costs exceed $5,000, you may have to **amortize** (spread out) the rest over 15 years — but that's a good problem to have. It means you're investing.

Step 3: Choose the Right Business Structure

There's no one-size-fits-all, but here's the real-world breakdown.

Sole Proprietor

- Easiest to start
- No separation between you and the business
- Uses your Social Security Number
- Filed on **Schedule C**

Best for: Test-driving your idea or early side hustles

LLC (Limited Liability Company)

- Adds legal protection
- Gets its own EIN (like a business SSN)
- Still filed as sole prop **unless you elect otherwise**

Best for: Freelancers, service providers, and product-based businesses who want to look and act legit

S-Corporation

- Pass-through entity, avoids self-employment tax on some income
- Requires payroll setup and more bookkeeping

- Must file **Form 2553** with the IRS

Best for: Business owners making over $50K profit who want to keep more and avoid SE tax

C-Corporation

- Separate legal and tax entity
- Subject to double taxation unless carefully managed
- Used mostly for larger companies or those seeking investors

Best for: Scalable startups, companies issuing shares, or advanced strategies

---

Step 4: Set Up The Essentials

If you're serious about your business, you need more than just a CashApp tag and an Instagram handle.

You need:

- **An EIN** – Get one for free at IRS.gov. No LLC required.
- **A business bank account** – Never mix business with personal.
- **A bookkeeping system** – QuickBooks, Wave, or a spreadsheet.
- **Basic legal structure** – DBA, LLC, or S-Corp, depending on your situation.
- **A strategy** – Even a simple one-page business plan helps you operate intentionally.

Step 5: Know When to Upgrade

Most businesses don't need to over-complicate things on day one. But here's when you know it's time to level up your structure:

- You're profiting **more than $50,000/year** — look at S-Corp options
- You're signing **contracts** or hiring others — get an LLC or higher
- You're spending more than you're tracking — get a bookkeeper

- You want to build **business credit or secure funding**

Real Talk: Start Smart So You Don't Have to Fix It Later

I've seen people lose thousands in missed deductions, delayed filings, legal fines, or simply looking unprofessional — all because they didn't want to spend $50 and 30 minutes setting things up the right way. That's not strategy. That's gambling.

Whether you're flipping sneakers, selling lashes, driving Uber, coaching online, or editing YouTube videos — you're in business now.

So move like it.

Business Starter Toolkit

From Day One.

"If you treat your hustle like a hobby, the IRS — and your bank account — will too."

1. Choose a Business Name

- Make sure it's unique in your state
- Check availability on domain and social media
- Optional: Register your DBA ("Doing Business As") if using a name different from your own

2. Get Your EIN (Employer Identification Number)

- Free and instant at irs.gov/ein
- Needed for business bank account, employees, S-Corp elections, and many apps/platforms
- Even if you're a sole proprietor, get an EIN — stop using your SSN for everything

3. Open a Business Bank Account

- Use your EIN and business name
- Keep personal and business money completely separate
- This makes bookkeeping easier and protects you legally

4. Choose Your Structure

- Sole Proprietor: Start immediately, file with Schedule C
- LLC: Register with your state, adds legal protection
- S-Corp: Elect after forming LLC or Corp (using Form 2553)
- C-Corp: Rare for small businesses, but useful for long-term planning or investors

5. Set Up Basic Bookkeeping

- Choose a system: QuickBooks, Wave, Notion, or a spreadsheet

- Track income, expenses, receipts, and mileage
- Review your numbers monthly — not just in tax season

6. Get a Business Email & Phone Number

- Use G Suite, Zoho, or ProtonMail for a professional domain
- Google Voice or Grasshopper for a dedicated business line

7. Register for Any Licenses or Permits

- Local city/county business license
- Sales tax permit (if selling products)
- Industry-specific licenses (cosmetology, notary, etc.)

8. Create a Basic Business Presence

- Social media profile(s)
- Website or landing page (even if it's just a free one)
- Email signature, logo, bio, and offer statement

9. Build a Document Folder

Create a Google Drive or Dropbox folder with:

- Articles of Organization (if LLC)
- EIN confirmation letter
- Receipts and statements
- Contracts and invoices
- Monthly financial snapshots

10. Start Tracking Deductions From Day One

- Use the Write-Off Tracker Template from Chapter 6
- Start building the habit now — don't wait until your first tax season

Optional but Powerful Add-Ons:

- Business insurance (liability, E&O, commercial auto, etc.)
- Bookkeeper or virtual assistant
- Business credit building steps

- Contracts and agreements (independent contractor templates, NDAs)

Reminder from Mr. Then:

Don’t overcomplicate the start. Just start right. You don’t need an MBA or a six-figure launch. You need structure, clarity, and a game plan. This toolkit gives you that.

Coming up next in Chapter 8: The Secrets of the Self-Employed

We’ll get into the nitty-gritty of self-employment tax, how to beat it legally, and why most freelancers are leaking money without realizing it.

Secrets of the Self-Employed

They tell you to work for yourself, but don't tell you about the 15.3% coming for your neck.

"Self-employment tax isn't the enemy — ignorance is."

The First Time You Realize You Owe
Most self-employed people have this moment:

- You make $40,000 freelancing or side hustling
- You feel great… until tax season
- The tax software says you owe $6,000 or more
- You stare at the screen wondering if it's broken

It's not.
That's self-employment tax, and if you don't plan for it, it hits like a brick.

What Is Self-Employment Tax?

It's how the IRS collects Social Security and Medicare taxes from people who work for themselves.
Employees split these taxes with their employer.
Self-employed individuals? You pay the full 15.3% yourself.
Breakdown:

- 12.4% for Social Security (up to a cap)
- 2.9% for Medicare (no cap)
- If you make over $200,000 (single), there's a 0.9% additional Medicare tax

You pay this on top of your regular income tax.
Example: The Math They Don't Teach You
Let's say you made $60,000 from your business.

- You get the standard deduction: -$15,000

- Taxable income: $45,000
- Federal income tax: ~$5,100
- Self-employment tax (15.3% of $60,000): $9,180

Your total tax bill: $14,280

This shocks people because there were no taxes withheld during the year. That's why you must treat self-employment income like it's not all yours.

How to Reduce Self-Employment Tax Strategically

Here's how the pros do it — legally and smart.

1. Business Deductions

The more legitimate business expenses you track and deduct, the lower your net income, and the less tax you pay.

Examples:

- Mileage
- Software
- Equipment
- Marketing
- Education
- Business use of home

Document everything. No guessing.

2. Contribute to a Retirement Plan

Open a SEP IRA or Solo 401(k). These let you lower your taxable income while saving for the future.

- SEP IRA: Contribute up to 25% of net income, max $69,000 (2024 limit)
- Solo 401(k): Employee + employer contribution combo

3. Switch to S-Corp (When the Time Is Right)

Once you're profiting over $50K–$75K, talk to your tax pro about electing S-Corp status.

Why? Because:

- You pay yourself a "reasonable salary" (which is taxed)
- The rest can be paid to you as distributions (which are not subject to self-employment tax)

This alone can save thousands per year if structured correctly.

4. Pay Quarterly Taxes

Avoid penalties by making estimated tax payments every quarter (Form 1040-ES)

Due Dates:

- April 15
- June 15
- September 15
- January 15 (of the next year)

Treat it like a bill. Set the money aside every month so tax season doesn't feel like an ambush.

Tools That Make Self-Employment Easier

You don't need to do this alone or manually. These tools help you stay organized and tax-ready:

- QuickBooks Self-Employed (mileage, income, receipts)
- Keeper Tax
- Everlance (for mileage tracking)
- Google Sheets (if you like control)
- TurboTax Self-Employed / TaxSlayer or a Tax Preparer like me (filing software)

Mr. Then's Real Talk

If you're self-employed and not planning ahead, you're walking into every year with a financial blindfold.

Self-employment is freedom — but only if you treat it like a business, not a hustle.

If you're making money without a strategy, the IRS is getting more of it than they deserve. Every dollar you don't track, plan for, or structure is a dollar they get to keep.

That ends now.

Quarterly Tax Prep Checklist

Stay ready so you don't have to get ready.

"Tax season isn't once a year. It's every quarter — if you're really in business."

Overview:
If you're self-employed, the IRS expects you to make estimated quarterly tax payments. Miss them, and you could owe penalties — even if you break even in April. This checklist helps you prepare, stay organized, and minimize the hit.
Quarterly Due Dates (20XX):

Quarter	Income Period	Payment Due Date
Q1	Jan 1 – Mar 31	April 15
Q2	Apr 1 – May 31	June 15
Q3	Jun 1 – Aug 31	September 15
Q4	Sep 1 – Dec 31	January 15 (20XX following Tax Year)

What to Do Each Quarter:

1. Update Your Books

- Reconcile income and expenses
- Review invoices and deposits
- Categorize deductions accurately

Tool Suggestions: QuickBooks, Wave, Excel, Notion, or a bookkeeper

2. Review Your Profit

- Calculate gross income
- Subtract business expenses
- Determine net profit for the quarter

Net profit is what you'll be taxed on — not gross.

3. Set Aside 25–30% of Net Profit

This covers:

- 15.3% Self-employment tax
- 10–15% Federal income tax (estimate)

Adjust based on your actual tax bracket or last year's return.

4. Make Your Estimated Payment (Form 1040-ES)

- Submit payment online at irs.gov/payments
- Or mail Form 1040-ES with a check
- Save the confirmation for your records

5. Log Key Receipts & Documents

- Business purchases
- Mileage logs
- Meal receipts (annotated with date, purpose, who)
- Home office expenses
- Subscription and software charges
- Retirement contributions (SEP IRA, Solo 401k)

6. Check in with Your Tax Pro (Optional but Wise)

- Ask if you should switch to S-Corp
- Review any new tax law changes
- Make sure you're not missing hidden deductions

Optional: End-of-Quarter Deep Clean

- Download bank statements
- Save all receipts into Google Drive or Dropbox
- Create a "Quarter [X] Tax Folder"
- Back up your tracker and bookkeeping records
- Note any large expenses or income spikes

Final Words from Mr. Then:

"If you're not treating taxes like part of your business, you're just winging it. And winging it is expensive."

Coming up in Chapter 9: Tax Tools They Don't Teach in School

We're unlocking the real power moves — entities, trusts, EINs, elections, and more.

Rules They Don't Teach in School

LLCs, S-Corps, Trusts, and the legal flexes that change the tax game.

"The IRS wrote the rules — wealthy people just actually read them."

The Game Isn't Rigged — You're Just Under-informed
Most people file taxes once a year, cross their fingers, and hope for a refund. Wealthy people? They structure their lives to win before the first dollar even hits their account.
These tools aren't just for millionaires. They're available to anyone with the knowledge and discipline to use them.
This chapter breaks down the heavy hitters.

1. LLC (Limited Liability Company)
What it is:
A legal entity that separates your business and personal finances.
Why it matters:

- Protects your personal assets
- Makes your business look legit
- Can be taxed as a sole prop, partnership, or elect S-Corp status

Who it's for:
Freelancers, service providers, and product-based business owners who want protection and professionalism.

Tax Impact:
By default, still taxed as a sole proprietor unless you make an S-Corp election.

2. S-Corporation (S-Corp)
What it is:
A tax classification, not a type of business. You "elect" S-Corp status by filing Form 2553 after forming an LLC or Corporation.
Why it matters:
- Avoids self-employment tax on part of your income
- Allows you to split income into reasonable salary (W-2) + owner distributions

Who it's for:
Business owners consistently profiting $50K+ annually
Tax Impact:
Huge savings on self-employment taxes. But comes with increased compliance:
- Must run payroll (can use Gusto, ADP, etc.)
- Must file corporate return (Form 1120S)

3. Trusts
What it is:
A legal arrangement that holds and manages assets for the benefit of someone else.
Why it matters:
- Avoids probate
- Creates generational wealth systems
- Can reduce estate taxes
- Offers privacy and asset protection

Types:
- Revocable Living Trust – Used for estate planning while you're alive
- Irrevocable Trust – Used for reducing tax liability and protecting assets from lawsuits

- Grantor vs. Non-Grantor Trusts – Control and taxability differences

Who it's for:
Anyone with assets, heirs, or goals beyond themselves
Tax Impact:
Trusts can be taxed at high rates if misused — but used strategically, they transfer wealth without getting destroyed by taxes.

4. Holding Companies

What it is:
A parent entity that owns other businesses or assets
Why it matters:

- Centralizes ownership
- Protects your core entity
- Separates liability across multiple businesses

Who it's for:
Multi-business owners or those expanding into real estate, licensing, or IP
Tax Impact:
Depends on how it's structured. Often combined with LLCs, S-Corps, or Trusts to build a tax-optimized empire.

5. EIN (Employer Identification Number)

What it is:
The Social Security Number for your business.
Why it matters:

- Needed to open business bank accounts
- Required to hire employees
- Keeps your personal SSN out of client/vendor paperwork

Who it's for:
Literally anyone running a business or planning to grow one

Tax Impact:
No tax benefit alone — but essential for structuring and separating finances.

6. QBI Deduction (Qualified Business Income)
What it is:
A 20% tax deduction for pass-through entities (sole props, partnerships, S-Corps)
Why it matters:

- Lowers your taxable income
- Only available through business income, not W-2

Who it's for:
Anyone with business income — up to $182,100 (single) or $364,200 (married filing jointly) in 2025 before it begins to phase out
Tax Impact:
Reduces taxable income by up to 20% — that's massive.

7. Retirement Accounts for Business Owners
Options:

- SEP IRA
- Solo 401(k)
- Defined Benefit Plans (advanced)

Why it matters:

- Deductions now, wealth later
- Shelter income from taxes while building long-term wealth

Tax Impact:
Could lower your taxable income by tens of thousands while investing for the future.
8. Family Income Shifting
What it is:
Paying your kids (or spouse) from your business for real work

Why it matters:

- Shifts income into lower tax brackets
- Makes use of your child's standard deduction

Rules:

- Must be legitimate work
- Must document hours, pay, and duties
- Use payroll or issue 1099 if over the threshold

Tax Impact:
Your child can earn up to $14,600 (standard deduction in 2025) tax-free. You deduct the expense — they don't pay tax.

Mr. Then's Real Talk:
The tax code is over 70,000 pages — and 90% of it is about how not to pay taxes when you do things right. The people who win at taxes aren't "cheating." They're using the same IRS rules that are available to everyone — they just read the playbook and ran the plays.
You now have the tools. Don't let this chapter sit as theory. Start implementing.

Tax Strategy Stack

The blueprint to keeping more, building faster, and staying audit-proof.

"The goal isn't just to pay less tax — it's to build smarter, grow faster, and never flinch when the IRS shows up."

LEVEL 1: Get Legit

- Get an EIN from the IRS (free at irs.gov)
- Open a business bank account (stop mixing funds)
- Choose a name and file your DBA or LLC
- Use basic bookkeeping (spreadsheet, app, or software)

Result: You're officially in business. IRS takes you more seriously. You now qualify for deductions.

LEVEL 2: Track Everything

- Start a deduction tracker (see Chapter 6)
- Track mileage, meals, supplies, subscriptions, software
- Save receipts digitally or in the cloud
- Reconcile monthly (income – expenses = taxable profit)

Result: You stay audit-ready, spot issues early, and minimize your taxable income.

LEVEL 3: Optimize for Tax Savings

- Deduct home office, vehicle, cell phone, internet
- Open a SEP IRA or Solo 401(k) for retirement deductions

- Pay your quarterly taxes to avoid penalties
- Review for QBI (20%) deduction eligibility

Result: You're no longer overpaying. Your system is smarter than most employees'.

LEVEL 4: Upgrade Your Entity

- Consider S-Corp election if profiting $50K+
- Split income between reasonable salary + owner distributions
- Run payroll using a legit system
- File Form 2553 with the IRS

Result: You reduce self-employment tax and unlock the next level of tax efficiency.

LEVEL 5: Family Tax Planning

- Hire your kids (age 7+) to work in your business
- Pay them legally and document their role
- Shift income to their 0% tax bracket
- Deduct their wages from your business income

Result: Family earns tax-free money, and you deduct it. Legal and smart.

LEVEL 6: Asset Protection + Legacy

- Set up a Revocable Living Trust
- Start building business credit and legal firewalls
- Create a holding company if you own multiple brands/assets
- Use irrevocable trusts for estate tax planning (with a pro)

Result: You protect what you've built, avoid probate, and build generational wealth.

Bonus Stack: Tax Pro Moves

- Use bonus depreciation and Section 179 for large asset purchases
- Run business retreats and document them properly

- Invest in tax-advantaged real estate
- Start preparing taxes in Q3, not Q1

Result: You go from playing defense to full-blown offense. You're now tax dangerous.

Mr. Then's Reminder:

"Don't try to skip to the top if you haven't mastered the bottom."

Structure before strategy. Strategy before scale. Keep stacking.

Bulletproof Your Tax Return

Avoid audits. Eliminate red flags. Protect your paper.

"You don't have to be scared of the IRS — if you stop filing like a rookie."

Why This Chapter Matters
Every year, thousands of people get audited, flagged, or hit with penalties — not because they cheated, but because they **filed sloppy, guessed too much, or triggered a red flag.**
We're not here to fear the IRS. We're here to file so clean, so solid, and so strategic that they move on to the next sucker.

What Actually Triggers an Audit?
The IRS doesn't have time to review every return. So, they use algorithms and AI to look for **outliers, patterns, and red flags**. Here's what lights them up:

- **High deductions compared to income** (e.g., $80K income, $65K deductions)
- **Excessive charitable donations** (especially if they don't match income)
- **Large Schedule C losses year after year** (especially without revenue)
- **Claiming 100% business use of your vehicle**
- **Mixing personal and business expenses**
- **Sudden spikes in income or deductions**
- **Incorrect Social Security numbers or math errors**
- **Too many dependents without documentation**
- **Frequent amended returns**

The more your return **stands out**, the more likely it is to be pulled for review.

The IRS Doesn't Care If You "Didn't Know"
Lack of knowledge doesn't get you out of penalties. In fact, the most dangerous thing you can file is a tax return with **a mix of confidence and confusion.**
So, let's bulletproof it.

---

10 Ways to Bulletproof Your Return

1. **Document Everything**
Receipts, mileage logs, invoices, bank statements, and proof of business use.
If you claim it, be ready to **show it.**

2. **Separate Business and Personal Finances**
No commingling. No "I think that was for work."
Use a dedicated business account and card. Period.

3. **Use Realistic Numbers**
Don't round everything to zeros or fives.
"$1,000 for meals," "$5,000 for supplies" — that looks lazy. IRS knows you're guessing.

4. **Don't Claim 100% Business Use of Anything (Unless It's True)**
If you're claiming 100% business use of your car, phone, or home, you better have proof.
Split usage = safer and more believable.

5. **File Electronically**
E-filing reduces errors, speeds up refunds, and creates a clear digital trail.

6. **Double Check Personal Info**

Misspelled names, wrong SSNs, outdated addresses — these small mistakes delay refunds and trigger notices.

7. **Report All Income (Even Cash and Zelle)**
1099 or not, the IRS expects you to report **everything**. They're ramping up tracking — especially for digital payments.

8. **Don't Claim Fake Dependents**
Yes, people still try it. And yes, the IRS is watching. Be able to prove relationship, residency, and support.

9. **Be Careful With Amended Returns**
Too many changes year after year? Looks suspicious. If you must amend, make sure it's backed by documents and logic.

10. **Hire a Pro (or Become One)**
If your return is getting more complex — stop guessing. The penalty for doing it wrong costs more than just paying for help.

Red Flag vs. Green Flag Examples

Move	IRS View
Deducting meals and mileage with notes and receipts	Green
Deducting 90% of rent, phone, and gas without proof	Red
Showing business profit and reinvesting in growth	Green
Reporting losses 3 years in a row with no real activity	Red
Filing early and accurately with digital documentation	Green

Move	IRS View
Filing last-minute with missing info and rough numbers	Red

Audit-Proofing = Wealth Protection
You worked for this money. You structured your business. You tracked your deductions. Don’t let it fall apart over poor filing habits.

An IRS audit isn’t the end of the world — but if your return is airtight, they’ll move on fast.
This is what wealthy people understand. **It’s not just about what you earn. It’s about how well you defend what you keep.**

The Refund Game Trap

If you're excited about your refund, you probably overpaid.

"A Tax Refund isn't a Blessing — it's a Correction." – Carlos Ariel Then

---

The Problem with Refund Culture
You've seen the memes:

- "Waiting on my tax refund like…"
- "When that refund hits and you're rich for two weeks"
- "It's refund season, not tax season"

Let's be real — people have been programmed to **celebrate giving the government an interest-free loan**, and getting some of it back.
A refund isn't extra money.
It's **your money**, returned late, without interest, after the IRS used it all year.

What a Refund Actually Is
When you file your taxes, you're comparing:

- What you **owe** in taxes based on your income
  vs.
- What you **already paid** through withholdings or estimated payments

If you paid more than you owed, you get a refund.
If you paid less, you owe.
That's it. There's no magic. No bonus. No secret gift.
It's **a reconciliation.**

The Math Most People Miss
Let's say:

- You earned $50,000

- You owed $6,500 in federal taxes
- Your job withheld $8,000

Your refund is **$1,500.**

But you overpaid all year — giving the IRS **extra cash every check.**

Now imagine:

- You adjusted your withholdings correctly
- You used that money to invest, save, or fund your business

You could've earned interest, started a business, or built savings.

Instead, you waited 12 months for a delayed deposit.

Why the Refund Mindset Keeps You Poor

- It encourages **financial passivity**
- It trains you to **rely on the IRS** for budgeting
- It hides poor tax planning
- It gives the illusion of a financial "win" that's really a **loss in time and opportunity cost**

The Refund Is Often a Symptom of a Bigger Problem

- You're **over-withholding** from your paycheck
- You don't know how to calculate **your true tax liability**
- You're not using legal strategies to **reduce taxes up front**
- You're **afraid to owe**, so you let the IRS hold your money "just in case"

The solution isn't "never get a refund."

The solution is **strategic control.**

Mr. Then's Refund Rule:

"If you're getting more than $2,000 back, you're probably giving up power somewhere else."

That money could've:

- Paid down high-interest debt

- Bought equipment for your business
- Gone into a Roth IRA or Solo 401(k)
- Covered quarterly taxes for your side hustle
- Built a cushion so you don't depend on tax season to breathe

---

How to Take Control

1. Adjust Your W-4 (If You're W-2)

Use the **IRS Withholding Estimator** or talk to a pro

Make sure your employer is withholding based on **your real life**, not generic defaults

2. Plan for Self-Employment Income

Use **quarterly payments**, not panic

Base your estimates on profit, not gross income

3. Track Year-Round

- Know your numbers monthly
- Anticipate what you'll owe
- Strategize before December, not in April

4. Set Refunds to Work

If you still get a refund — use it intentionally:

- Start an emergency fund
- Reinvest into income-generating activities
- Pay annual business expenses in one hit
- Fund your retirement

Redefining Winning

Winning isn't a big refund.

Winning is **keeping more of your money all year**, using it to build, grow, and invest — then filing a clean return that confirms you already had it handled.

You don't need the IRS to "bless" you.

You need a better system.

Coming up in Chapter 12: **Tax Season is Year-Round**

Let's stop reacting every April and start planning every January. This is where real freedom begins.

Refund/Withholding Calculator

Find out how much of your own money you've been letting the IRS babysit.

"Your refund is a mirror — not a reward."

Instructions: Use this to estimate how much you overpaid and what that money could've done if you'd had it all year.

Step	Input	Example	Your Number
1. Total Tax Owed for the Year (Line 24 of 1040)	—	$7,200	
2. Total Federal Withholding or Estimated Payments (Line 25d of 1040)	—	$9,000	
3. Subtract Step 1 from Step 2	= Refund	$1,800	
4. Divide Refund by 12 (Monthly Over-payment)	—	$150/mo	

Step	Input	Example	Your Number
5. Multiply Monthly Over-payment by 1.05 (5% compounding)	= Potential Invested Value	$1,957	

What You Could've Done With That Monthly Refund:

- **$150 into a Roth IRA** = $1,800–$2,000 per year in growing retirement
- **$150 toward debt** = Saved hundreds in interest
- **$150 into a business** = Domain, ads, software, branding
- **$150 into a savings account** = Emergency fund in 12 months

---

Withholding Worksheet (W-2 Workers Only)

Use this to tighten up your paycheck and stop overpaying.

Step 1: Grab Your Pay Stub

- Look at your **YTD Federal Withholding**
- Look at your **gross pay** so far

Step 2: Estimate Total Yearly Withholding

Monthly Federal Withholding	$__________
x 12 months	= $__________

Compare this to:

- Your actual tax owed from last year
- Your expected tax owed this year (based on income, filing status, and deductions)

Step 3: Identify the Gap

Expected Tax Owed	$__________
Minus Expected Withholding	$__________
= Over-payment or Underpayment	$__________

Step 4: Update Your W-4 If Needed
You can submit a new **W-4** to your employer at any time.
Use the **IRS Withholding Estimator**:
irs.gov/individuals/tax-withholding-estimator
Adjust:

- **Line 4a**: Other income (side hustle, interest, etc.)
- **Line 4b**: Deductions (to reduce taxable income)
- **Line 4c**: Extra withholding per paycheck (if you're playing catch-up)

Final Tip:
If you consistently get a $2,000+ refund, you're not "winning" — you're just letting the IRS use your money all year for free.

Use these tools to **balance your withholding**, plan for self-employment, and turn tax season into a **confirmation** — not a surprise.

Tax Season Is Year-Round

The people who win at taxes don't wait for the calendar. They plan like it's always April.

"If your taxes are a surprise, your money probably is too."

The Problem with "Tax Season"
The phrase "tax season" is part of the trap.
It makes people believe:

- Taxes are a once-a-year event
- You can ignore everything until March
- You'll figure it out when you get your W-2 or 1099

But the truth is, the people who come up every year — who owe less, keep more, and file clean — aren't reacting in April. They're planning in **January, July, and every month in between.**

What Year-Round Tax Strategy Looks Like
January – March: **Organize + Project**

- Set up bookkeeping systems
- Estimate income and expenses for the year
- Make adjustments to your W-4 or quarterly payments
- If self-employed: start clean, open business accounts, and track from Day 1

April – June: **File + Reassess**

- File your return early, not in panic
- Pay Q1 estimated taxes by April 15
- Review last year's return for missed opportunities
- Check your deductions and start a new strategy list

July – September: **Mid-Year Review**

- Recalculate income projections
- Make Q2 and Q3 estimated payments
- Adjust withholdings again if your job or life changed
- Revisit mileage logs, expenses, and any gaps in records

October – December: **Plan for the Finish**

- Spend intentionally before year-end
- Make retirement contributions (Solo 401k, SEP IRA)
- Purchase business equipment/tools if needed
- Lock in deductions with final investments or write-offs
- Book your consultation if you work with a tax pro

Habits That Make Taxes Easy

- Keep digital receipts and upload them weekly
- Use a mileage app year-round — don't guess
- Review income and expenses monthly
- Stay current with IRS updates (yes, they change stuff every year)
- Create a recurring **"money meeting"** on your calendar — once a month or quarterly

---

Tax Strategy Is Wealth Strategy

The goal isn't just to avoid an audit.

It's to **reclaim control** over one of your biggest expenses — taxes.

People budget groceries.

They budget gas.

But they leave taxes to chance — and then wonder why they can't get ahead.

You don't need to be an accountant.

You just need to treat taxes like **a key part of your business and life**, not an afterthought.

Mr. Then's Real Talk:

"You shouldn't be surprised by your taxes. You should be able to predict them within a few hundred dollars."
That's the kind of clarity that builds:

- Financial confidence
- Long-term wealth
- Real freedom

When you own your tax game, you unlock **options**.
And options are the real flex.

When it Hits the Fan - Tax Resolution

Owe the IRS? Here's how to fight back and come out on top.

"You're not in a tax problem— you're in tax situation. " - Carlos Ariel Then

---

Don't Panic. Just Play Smart.
Most people who owe the IRS think they're screwed — but they're not. The tax code is built with **escape routes**. If you're in debt, overwhelmed, or avoiding those scary letters, this chapter is your *game plan.*
We're going to cover:

- The real options for resolving your tax debt
- How long the IRS can actually come after you
- How to negotiate, delay, or **settle for less**
- What forms to file, and when to **stay silent**

Step 1: Understand Your IRS Status
Before you can fix the problem, you have to **face it.**
Request your transcripts at irs.gov/account
Check:

- **Wage & Income Transcripts**
- **Account Transcripts**
- **Return Transcripts**
- **CSED dates** (Collection Statute Expiration Dates)

You'll see:

- What years are missing
- How much you really owe
- When the IRS assessed the debt
- How close you are to the 10-year expiration window

Step 2: The IRS Clock Does Run Out

Here's the sauce: **The IRS only has 10 years to collect** from the date of assessment. That's called the **CSED** (Collection Statute Expiration Date).

If your debt is:

- **Past 10 years old** from assessment date = **Expired**
- **Close to expiring** = You might want to stall (smartly)
- Still new? You've got time — and leverage

Pauses the clock:

- Bankruptcy
- Offer in Compromise submission
- Installment Agreement negotiation
- Leaving the country
- Requests for Innocent Spouse Relief

You need to know your dates **before** you agree to anything.

Step 3: Choose Your Strategy

1. **Installment Agreement (Payment Plan)**

For people who can afford to pay, just not all at once.

- File **Form 9465**
- IRS allows up to **72 months (6 years)** to pay it down
- **Interest and penalties** keep running
- If you owe **under $50K**, it's automatic with minimal documentation

Bonus Tip: You can still negotiate penalties *after* getting on a plan (abatement requests).

---

2. **Offer in Compromise (OIC)**

This is how you **settle your tax debt for less** than you owe.

But it's not for everyone. The IRS looks at:

- Your **income**

- Your **assets**
- Your **expenses**
- Your ability to pay over time

If you can prove they're unlikely to collect the full amount before the 10 years runs out, they'll accept a lower offer.

You'll need:

- **Form 656**
- **Form 433-A (OIC)** — this is your full financial disclosure
- $205 application fee (unless you're low income)
- First payment (or monthly payments if paying over time)

Pro Tip: This is where you bring in a professional if the numbers are complicated. A properly prepared OIC = serious leverage.

---

3. **Currently Not Collectible (CNC)**

Can't afford anything? You may qualify for CNC status.

That means:

- The IRS **acknowledges your hardship**
- **Freezes collections**
- No wage garnishment or bank levies (for now)

They'll revisit your situation in **12–24 months**, but during that time:

- The **10-year clock keeps ticking**
- You have breathing room to strategize or fix your finances

File: Form **433-F** or **433-A**

Step 4: Penalty Abatement — Yes, You Can Ask

The IRS hands out **penalties like Halloween candy** — but many can be removed if you:

- Have **reasonable cause**
- Are a **first-time offender**

- Fix the issue proactively

Use:

- **Form 843** – Claim for Refund and Request for Abatement
- Write a clear, respectful **explanation** of what caused the delay
- Attach documentation (hospital records, divorce, disaster, COVID, etc.)

You'd be surprised how often this works — especially if you stay respectful and honest.

Step 5: Get Representation (When It's Bigger Than You)

If you owe more than **$25K**, have a **levy or lien**, or are **being audited** — don't do it alone.

You can authorize:

- **Enrolled Agents (EA)**
- **CPAs**
- **Tax Attorneys**

Use **Form 2848 (Power of Attorney)** so they can talk to the IRS on your behalf.

They can:

- Pull transcripts and analyze your CSEDs
- Submit OICs, payment plans, penalty abatements
- Negotiate settlements you probably won't get on your own

Mr. Then's Final Resolution Truth:

"The IRS wants your money — not your life. If you communicate, document, and play smart, you can settle."

IRS Survival Checklist:

- Pull your IRS transcripts
- Know your CSED
- Choose your strategy (Installment, OIC, CNC)

- Don’t miss deadlines
- File any missing returns
- Get help if it’s over your head
- Keep receipts of every payment and form submission

Tax Resolution Guide

The Official "I Owe the IRS" Playbook

"The IRS has rules. Learn them, and you stop being scared. Use them, and you start winning."

Step 1: Check Your IRS Status

Before you do anything, you need to know:

- How much you owe
- For which years
- What your **Collection Statute Expiration Date (CSED)** is
- If you've filed all required returns

How to Check:

- Go to: irs.gov/account
- Create/Log into your ID.me account
- Pull:
  - **Account Transcript**
  - **Wage & Income Transcript**
  - **Return Transcript**

Pro Tip: The IRS can't collect forever — they usually have **10 years from the date of assessment** (CSED). Don't ignore that.

Step 2: Know Your Options

1. **Installment Agreement (Payment Plan)**

Make monthly payments on your balance.

- File **Form 9465** (or apply online)
- No financials needed if balance is **under $50K**
- Standard terms: 72 months
- Still accrues interest + penalties, but stops collection actions

Good for: People who can pay monthly without hardship

---

2. **Offer in Compromise (OIC)**
Settle for less than you owe if you can prove you can't pay.

- Submit **Form 656** + **Form 433-A (OIC)**
- Requires full financial disclosure
- IRS calculates your **Reasonable Collection Potential (RCP)**
- If accepted, you wipe out the rest of the debt

Fee: $205 (waived for low income)
Strategy: Keep assets low and prove hardship to improve approval odds.
Good for: People with limited income/assets + high tax debt

---

3. **Currently Not Collectible (CNC) Status**
IRS agrees to pause collection if you can't afford to pay anything right now.

- File **Form 433-F** or **433-A**
- You still owe, but **no levies, garnishments, or payment demands**
- Reviewed every 1–2 years

Good for: Temporarily broke or in financial hardship

---

4. **Partial Payment Installment Agreement (PPIA)**
A middle ground — pay monthly but less than the full balance.

- Must file **433-A**
- IRS agrees to collect smaller amounts over time
- Remaining debt may expire due to statute of limitations

Good for: People who can pay *some*, but not all

Step 3: Penalty Abatement
If you've been hit with penalties, you may be able to get them **reduced or erased**.

Options:

- **First-Time Penalty Abatement** (clean record)
- **Reasonable Cause Abatement** (illness, natural disaster, etc.)

Form:

- **Form 843** – Claim for Refund and Request for Abatement
- Include a **detailed written explanation**

Good for: Anyone who missed a payment or filing due to life events

---

Step 4: Understand IRS Collections

- The IRS **cannot** seize your property without notice
- They **must** send:
    - CP14 (balance due)
    - CP504 (intent to levy)
    - LT11 (Final Notice of Intent to Levy)
- You have the right to **appeal** any collection attempt

Step 5: Know the 10-Year Rule

The IRS has 10 years from the **date of assessment** to collect a tax debt.

That includes:

- Filing the return
- IRS making changes and issuing a bill

Once that time is up — **you're off the hook.**

BUT: The clock **pauses** if you:

- File bankruptcy
- Submit an OIC
- Request CNC
- Leave the country
- File certain appeals

Good Strategy: If you're close to the 10-year mark, play defense and stall (legally).

Resolution Forms Cheat Sheet

Purpose	**Form**
Payment Plan	Form 9465
Offer in Compromise	Form 656
Financial Disclosure for OIC	Form 433-A (OIC)
Penalty Abatement	Form 843
Power of Attorney (Tax Pro)	Form 2848
Request IRS Transcripts	Online or Form 4506-T

Optional but Powerful Tools

- IRS Withholding Estimator (to avoid future problems)
- IRS Direct Pay: irs.gov/payments
- CAF (Centralized Authorization File) for tax pros
- Taxpayer Advocate Service if you feel stuck: https://www.taxpayeradvocate.irs.gov/

Final Words from Mr. Then:

"The IRS wants your money, not your soul. You just have to show up, respond, and play the long game."
This isn't about being perfect — it's about **being strategic**, staying calm, and knowing **they can't collect what you don't legally owe, and they can't chase you forever.**
Now you've got the blueprint.
Time to move like a tax boss — even in survival mode.

The Wealth Code — How the Rich Use Taxes

They're not just avoiding taxes. They're building empires with the money you're handing to the IRS.

"The rich don't run from taxes. They structure around them. And they use the tax code like a cheat code."

Stop Thinking Taxes Are the Problem
Taxes aren't the problem — **not knowing how to use them is.**
You've been taught to:

- Avoid audits
- Get a refund
- Hope for the best

But the wealthy don't play that game. They understand that the tax code isn't just a bill — it's a blueprint. And if you follow the blueprint, **you win by design**.

---

1. Real Estate = Tax-Free Money (If You Know the Moves)
This is the **#1 tax tool** for wealth.

- **Depreciation** lets you deduct a portion of your property's value every year — even if it's gaining value.
- **Cost segregation** breaks your building into parts (roof, appliances, carpet) to accelerate those deductions.
- **1031 Exchanges** let you sell and defer taxes if you reinvest into another property.
- **Borrowing against equity** = tax-free income. That HELOC? That refi cash? The IRS doesn't touch it.

The rich don't flip homes. They flip **equity** into more property while avoiding capital gains. You can too.

---

2. Buy Assets with Pre-Tax Dollars

Smart business owners don't spend money. They **allocate** pre-tax dollars.

Examples:

- Vehicle for your business? Deductible.
- Camera for your content? Deductible.
- Home office furniture? Deductible.
- Conference travel? Deductible.

Section 179 lets you deduct the full cost of qualifying equipment the year you buy it.

Bonus depreciation? That's extra juice — letting you write off even more.

---

3. Stack Entities for Power + Protection

Wealthy people don't operate everything under one name. They build **structures**.

- **LLC** for operations
- **S-Corp** for payroll and tax reduction
- **Holding company** for brand or asset ownership
- **Trust** for privacy and inheritance
- **C-Corp** (when needed) for reinvesting income

Your job is to **move money legally** between entities to minimize taxes, protect assets, and build generational control.

---

4. Use Life Insurance Like a Bank

Yeah, you heard right. Life insurance — but not the "basic $15/month" kind.

The wealthy use:

- **Indexed Universal Life (IUL)**
- **Whole Life with cash value**
- **Private placement life insurance (PPLI)** (for the ultra-wealthy)

They:

- Build **tax-deferred cash value**
- Borrow against it **tax-free**
- Pass it on **tax-free** under IRS code 101(a)

You don't have to love insurance — but you better understand how it's used as a **tax-free vault.**

---

5. Retirement Accounts Are Wealth Shields

You've heard of IRAs and 401(k)s. But the real plays are:

- **Solo 401(k)** with Roth option = save now and later
- **Backdoor Roth IRAs** = legal way around income limits
- **SEP IRAs** = big deductions for high earners
- **Self-directed IRAs** = invest in real estate, crypto, and more — **tax-free**

The rich max out these tools **early and aggressively.** You should too.

---

6. Shift Wealth — Not Just Income

Here's how the rich **move money down the line**:

- **Gift up to $18,000 per person per year**, tax-free
- Use **family LLCs** to control wealth while lowering taxable value
- Create **irrevocable trusts** to lock assets in while removing them from your estate
- **Dynasty trusts** = wealth that lasts 100+ years and skips multiple generations of estate tax

This is how people pass down **millions without letting Uncle Sam touch it.**

---

7. Taxes Are About Timing — Play the Long Game

- Shift income to **low-income years** (take distributions when you're in a lower bracket)
- Time asset sales to **capitalize on long-term gains**

- **Accelerate deductions** in high-income years (pay for that retreat or software now)
- **Delay income** when needed (invoice next year, defer contracts)

It's not always about the rate — it's about the **timing**.
And the wealthy are masters of timing.

Mr. Then's Wealth Truth:
"Your tax strategy isn't just about paying less — it's about using the tax code to build more."
That's the **Wealth Code**.
Once you realize that every deduction, deferment, and structure is a tool — not a loophole — you stop fearing taxes. You start using them.

Ready for the Mic Drop?
Coming up next — **Chapter 15: Final Word — You've Been Played Long Enough**
No more getting finessed by a system you were never taught. Let's talk legacy, freedom, and flipping the script — for good.

You've Been Taxed Your Whole Life

This game was never about taxes. It was about control. Now it's time to take that back. You're in control now.

"You can keep filing the way they taught you… or you can flip the script and never look back."

Let me say it plainly:
You were never meant to win the tax game.
You were meant to:

- Go to school
- Get a job
- File a W-2
- Be grateful for a refund
- Stay scared of audits
- And never ask too many questions

Meanwhile, the wealthy were using the same tax code to:

- Write off their lifestyle
- Hire their kids
- Buy real estate tax-free
- Use LLCs and S-Corps like armor
- Move millions without blinking

You didn't fail.
You were never taught.
And that ends now.

This Book Isn't Just a Guide — It's Permission

- Permission to stop overpaying
- Permission to track your life and deduct it
- Permission to file smarter, not harder

- Permission to take your business seriously
- Permission to build generational wealth — on your own terms

If you're reading this right now, understand something:

- You are no longer "hoping" for a refund.
- You are no longer afraid of the IRS.
- You are no longer waiting until tax season to handle your money.

You're moving differently now.

What Happens Next?

Here's what you do after you close this book:

- Print the deduction tracker
- Set up your business structure
- Get your EIN if you don't have one
- Open a business bank account
- Review your last 2 tax returns for missed money
- Create a system — or hire someone who has one
- Revisit this book **before** the year ends — not after tax season starts

---

Mr. Then's Challenge to You:

Don't let this book sit on your shelf.

Don't let this information be "interesting."

Don't just feel inspired — **get in motion.**

Because I promise you this: Every dollar you don't track, structure, or protect…

The IRS will gladly keep.

But every dollar you understand?

That's yours to grow, multiply, pass down, and control forever.

Final Word:

"Don't Tax Me" was never just about forms, numbers, or refunds.

It was a statement of power.

A decision to stop being played.
A declaration that **you know better now — and you're doing better too.**
You just flipped the script.
Now go flip your whole entire legacy.
- Mic drop

About the Author

Carlos Ariel Then didn't plan to become a player in the tax strategy game — the game chose him.
It started back in college at the University of Rhode Island. One day, a friend saw Carlos casually doing his own taxes and asked, "Yo, can you do mine? I'll pay you $50." It was a basic 1040 return. Fifteen minutes later, Carlos had the fastest $50 he'd ever made, and something clicked. That was the spark.
What did he do next? In true hustler fashion, he pulled up to the school library and made *every single computer* homepage his website. Aggressive? Maybe. Effective? Absolutely. A slap on the wrist followed, but so did the bag. He made a **ton of money**, lost a bunch of it, spent most of it unnecessarily, and learned some *very expensive lessons* — but never stopped leveling up.
Fast forward: it's been over **10 years** and Carlos is still in the game, sharpening his blade and stacking wins. He's guided thousands through the tax system, credit, business, cleaned up messy finances, and showed folks how to stop leaving money on the table. Currently studying to become an **Enrolled Agent (EA)** — the highest credential the IRS awards — he's writing this book while preparing to add that next weapon to his arsenal.
Now, as the founder of **Mr Then Consulting LLC**, Carlos brings bold tax strategy, credit repair, business coaching, and unapologetic financial education to the masses. He doesn't believe in gate-keeping game — he believes in **financial awakening**.
From flipping refunds in dorm rooms to flipping the script on how we understand taxes — this is Mr. Then.

Need Help?
Let's Talk.

Whether you're drowning in tax debt, trying to launch your business, or just looking for someone who actually *gets it* — I'm here.

I've made it my life's work to **study money** the way others study medicine or law.

Not just for me — but for **people who look like me**.
People who came from where I came from.
People who were never taught this sh*t in school.

What I Do (for Real)

Tax Prep & Strategy

From basic returns to advanced tax planning, side hustles, self-employment, real estate, and LLC setups. I don't just file — I **build game plans**.

IRS Problem Solver

If you owe back taxes, haven't filed, or are scared of those letters — I've got you.
Payment plans, Offers in Compromise, CNC status… I know the plays.

Business Coaching

Whether you're starting from scratch or scaling up, I help you **build structure, automate, and grow** with intention.

Certified Life Coaching

Because the truth is, most money problems aren't about money.
They're about mindset, boundaries, trauma, and clarity.
And I'm trained to help you work through all of that.

Financial Guidance for the Culture
I'm not here for performative professionalism. I'm here for **transformation**.
I want more millennial first-gens, creatives, side hustlers, and everyday builders to win.

Real Talk:
You don't have to figure all this out alone.
You don't have to be perfect.
You just have to **start with someone who gives a damn**.
That's me.
Let's work.

Ready to connect?
Email: carlos@mrthen.biz
Website: www.mrthen.biz
Social: @mr_then
Book a Call: bit.ly/mrthen-appt

This book was just the beginning. The rest of the story? You write it.
And if you want someone in your corner, guiding the way —
I'm here when you're ready.
— *Carlos Ariel Then*
Your Bilingual Tax Expert, Business Coach & Life Strategist
"Mr. Then is your Friend."

www.ingramcontent.com/pod-product-compliance
Lightning Source LLC
LaVergne TN
LVHW090329210926
848480LV00004B/1351